**If You Have Never
Surrendered
You Have Never Loved!**

If You Have Never Surrendered You Have Never Loved!

A guide to successful love for single or married people.

Deon L de Jongh

iUniverse, Inc.

New York Lincoln Shanghai

If You Have Never Surrendered You Have Never Loved!
A guide to successful love for single or married people.

iUniverse, Inc.

For information address:
iUniverse, Inc.
2021 Pine Lake Road, Suite 100
Lincoln, NE 68512
www.iuniverse.com

ISBN: 0-595-26888-9

Printed in the United States of America

Contents

ACKNOWLEDGEMENT

I would foremost like to thank God for having guided me through my times of trial and tribulation when all seemed lost. I encourage each person to find his/her source of strength in a higher existence to carry them through the impossible, where man fails.

Through the path of my own experiences, I have written this book to possibly help guide others to safer waters, through stormy relationships, and free them from that prison of loneliness. Every day I acknowledge and accept my mortality and mistakes I have made in the past to come to this stage of understanding and realization of what love was, is, and can be.

I would like to thank my parents, Leslie and Joan de Jongh from beautiful Cape Town, South Africa. They taught me the Old School ways of "Love": to respect my elders, to have tolerance for differences, treasure family, be truthful, honest, and have dignity through humility for all. They showed me to have compassion and charity for those who are less fortunate, and, more importantly, to realize that life does not guarantee happiness. The value of honesty and love I grew up in became my cornerstone to life.

I would like to thank my friend, confidant and trusted love Jessica Prior for making the submission of this book possible. She did the unique and beautiful cover illustration with a special message therein. She also did the editing of this book to its last revision un-selfishly. I thank you from the bottom of my heart.

To the staff of iUniversal Publishers, thank you for your professional care and dedication to success. Sincere appreciation for what you have done.

Lastly, I would like to thank all the anonymous friends that made this book possible through their contributions and shared thoughts.

PROLOGUE

Everywhere you go in the world today, there is a city metropolis or town filled with people in pursuit of family, fame, wealth, love, and happiness.

One such city is the fashion and business capital, New York City, also known as the Big Apple. This is the place where dreams come true, business deals close, and where millions of dwellers make a living and find shelter in the shadows of the majestic skyscrapers, echoing the names of Broadway and Times Square.

Observing from a distance, one sees thousands of people walking the streets like worker ants with the modern attire of electronic gadgets, emphasizing the need for progress and technology to stay abreast in this modern and ever-changing world.

Yet, somehow when you walk amongst them, their faces tell a different story as to what the city life offers in a nutshell. An almost cynical contrast illuminates the true distraught features of the most promising Wall Street broker, hopeful lovers, or aspiring artist.

What does this all mean? The answer is easy. A city crowded to capacity, bubbling over with financial, social, and extravagant events, yet filled with dismayed and lonely people who hate their jobs and dread potential relationships.

I will attempt to bring some form of hope and perspective to this illness that plagues every metropolis and town, where the air should be enhanced with the joy of love and smiles, yet is over-cast with just the opposite. Not only will this be looked at in depth, but explained in basic terms how to overcome the effects of this condition.

This book will serve as direct guide and tool for single, engaged, or married people, those either searching for success and love, or finding happiness. I will be direct and give realistic solutions you can deal with and relate to.

One's own experience is the best teacher, so this book is com-piled based upon my own understanding and the lives of others who have either lost or found true love. Read with insight, and I sincerely hope that this will give you a better indication of how to find love, keep it, and surrender to it with the confidence of knowing yourself.

INTRODUCTION

Finding that elusive Mr. or Miss. Right or recipe to a committed relationship or marriage will be the goal and ambition of many who explore the relationship scene. Irrespective of sexual orientation, the never-ending quest for peace of mind, trust, and attaining love becomes the aspiration of every individual. This is a guide to achieving just that-finding yourself, understanding your relationships, and preparing you with the tools of the trade to find happiness, heal from past experiences, and achieve acceptance of your current status-whether you are single or not.

Although we can live within a reasonable existence without a partner, we all yearn for a sense of belonging deep within ourselves. Many choose to devote their time to work, or any activity, rather than in the pursuit of happiness with a partner. Why? Either by choice or by past pain inflicted through infidelity, broken trust, abuse, isolation, or any condition bringing about the condition to be "Alone". Feeling that sense of belonging gives us "Purpose" that extends to our livelihood in how we go through life and deal with the inevitable condition of death that awaits us all at the end of life's journey.

Making mistakes in a relationship and facing the failures will be an unchangeable condition as long as we are human and deal with different people in the trials and tribulation of life. Our mistakes can bring personal shame, disaster to the most promising relationships, or be the bonding agent of learning that endures through love that will stand the test of time.

This book will assist you in the re-evaluation of you current relationship, in the pursuit of happiness for the "Self", or with a promising partner. Concerning marriage and divorce, this book will also help you understand the trial or the inevitable step that leads up to the heartache and sorrow accompanying it.

The Rule is… "If you Chose to Love…Love your Choice."…If not, change your life for the better through spiritual stability and realistic choices based upon the unselfishness of respect and understanding of mutual benefit for you and those affected by the choices. Love is precious…and so is life…treasure and share it, and gather in this world that which can not be purchased with the material objects of this world: friendship, understanding, compassion, humility, respect, and love.

I strongly and sincerely recommend that you start from Chapter 1 and read each chapter in order rather than jumping ahead.

I wish you, the reader, all the very best in whichever choices you make in the name of love.

Remember to think clearly and realistically based upon the faith of conditions and then acceptance of the task at hand, bearing and understanding the benefits or consequences of our actions.

CHAPTER 1

"Definitions of Love"

"Definitions of Love"

Love can be explained in many languages and different cultures, yet it has a core of common interest all beings share. One can love a task, food, possession, job, or anything related to experiencing the adoring emotion thereof. Love can be plutonic, real, superficial, pre-arranged, or narcissistic. Love can be that oasis of seclusion where one can feel safe and comfortable.

In my own opinion, love is a mind-state of care, appreciation, enjoyment, happiness, value, serenity, affection, charity, and compassion from which an emotion can be derived or obtained from mutual interest of those involved.

Let's hear what some New Yorkers have to say.

Senior citizen married over 30 years:

"My goodness…our generation's love is everything it said in the Bible…"

Single, divorced mother her 30's:

"Love is the closest thing one can feel in respect to the divine and true purpose of humanity."

Divorced man in his 30's:

"Love sucks!!! With all the broken relationships, love has become overrated and lost its true purpose of romance."

Engaged woman in her 20's:

"Love is undefinable…for it varies too much in meaning from one person to another."

Single man in his 20's:

"There is no guarantee of happiness in the word love, because of all the broken relationships."

Teenager:

"I don't know...I've learned from my parents that love endures."

Many New Yorkers had much to say about love but many did not live the tale they told.

"To talk the talk is easy...but to walk the walk is another matter altogether."

Let's look at love in its unique facet and various stages of perspectives:

A) *Mutual Love*: This emotion applies to two beings who are able to display and give affection in an intellectual and equal natural manner. For example: owner and pet or between two people.

Understanding of this relationship lies within the mutual indication of intention to stimulate and explore a bond of friendship.

The display of affection in private or public places largely depends on the mood and intention or either partner to connect or feel secure. There is no greater feeling in love as when it is mutual. Those who experience love at first sight feel that adrenaline rush of awe when first encountering that mate or partner. That determination is foremost made by natural selection of appearance. Our preferences set that standard or level of interest we might have towards the opposite sex-whether it be age, build, ethnic background, or dress. The criteria vary from one person to another. Appearance comprises an integral part of the mating game and thus is a first line of evaluation.

What is appealing to a native aborigine in Australia might not be so appealing to a European in the western world. So, the selection preference takes place long before we reach adulthood.

The determining factors are geographically and socially instilled in a child through parental preference in cultural roots.

This creates a dilemma for foreigners traveling abroad. How? A mate of their own culture in another country might have had different exposure to the freedom of living in respect to the customs still practiced. So caution needs to be taken on both sides when approaching a potential mate.

The obvious signs of positive response is locked in the mutual "gaze of acknowledgement" then followed by a smile. That still does not indicate affection of mutual pursuit. The man or woman can only confirm their understanding through communication of verbal agreement. A soft and sincere smile of friendliness can wrongfully be mistaken by a love-sick puppy about to make a nasty discovery.

The Golden Rules Is: "Don't assume…ask! Nothing beats conversation.

This risk is all too well-displayed in nature when the female scorpion and black widow spider could eat their mate if unwelcome approach is pursued.

As long as the feelings are mutual, a channel of communication can lead to further endeavors.

B) *Platonic Love:* This emotion coincides very much to the superficial aspect of many relationships. In this relationship there is not steadfast belief in a shared understanding. Platonic love indicates the emotional portion of a relationship where there is no definite arrangement or long-term commitment. Partners in such a relationship do not concern themselves with the in-depth aspects of relations. Either one can leave the relationship with no remorse or feeling of guilt. Platonic love is normally prone to infidelity and self interest.

C) *Gizmo Love:* Gizmo is a term I like to use for the small devices and peripherals that so many city dwellers equip themselves with to stay in the loop of technology for the communication era. Gizmo love exists between two people who schedule and organize their life around their diaries, phone calls, palm pilots, business meetings, and social gatherings. Heaven forbid they ignore all the abovementioned and just go for a normal uninterrupted walk or romantic dinner without their colleagues or clique of friends.

D) *New Age Love:* In recent years, people have re-discovered holistic healing and spiritual awakening through yoga and meditative ways to relieve the stresses of everyday life, as well as finding life and purpose through a unique cultivation and cleansing of mind, body, and spirit. People in this mainstream arena flock to gatherings or places of tranquility to either discover themselves or find that partner with a similar passion.

When they meet and interact, their union and purpose of life becomes one and brings a higher purpose to their everyday existence. With that love, they set out to understand themselves in a committed relationship of newly founded understanding based upon the ancient and spiritual ways of self-realization.

E) *Religious and Political Love:* The fundamentals of this love are based upon the respective common religious and political affiliation. Whether conformed to for the sake of family or community, the relationship will carry the ways of traditions and generations. In many communities and family households, the children share the common interest with the parents and then pursue a mate with the same said understanding. Many couples will give up the most promising of relationships to satisfy this criteria of love. The determining factor to religious love has its core based upon the scriptural love reference in 1 Corinthians 13 v. 4—7. The political aspect entails all of the current and ever-changing climates in the political arena of interest or importance.

F) *True Love:* Complete and trustworthy surrender of all devices with respect to realistic and mutual approach to feelings and goals.

CHAPTER 2

"Matters Concerning Trust"

"Matters Concerning Trust"

Trust is that strong yet fragile substance that gives rise to our honorable intentions and integrity in society. Trust is also our free choice to selectively confide in another the depth of our innermost vulnerability, concerns, doubts, fears, and secrets, in the hopes that they would be treasured and shared exclusively between one's self and one's partner.

To trust is never an easy thing to do once we have encountered betrayal in some form or another. The true essence and substance of a relationship is first and foremost based upon these previous encounters. From that, mutual respect, understanding, and love can either grow or whither.

Many that have endured the trials of a relationship or have aspirations to engage in one can testify of its importance. Over a number of years, unbroken trust binds the relationship to an enduring bond of affection and completeness. This, however, does not guarantee trust for all times. It can only be so if mutualy respected and treasured. There is a certain pattern of trust that occurs during growing relationships:

Selective Aspiring Trust:

Singles in or searching for a relationship where they can trust their new partner with selected information about them, seeing where it will go from there. During the relationship spot-checks will be made to determine the further life expectancy of trust.

Confident Trust:

After a lengthy relationship, the trust factor proceeds to the next level where the couple either moves in together, has a spare set of apartment keys, or shares the financial aspects of a commited relationship.

Contractual Trust:

Before the "happy" couple pledge their vows at church, they first make a pit-stop at the lawyers office to sign a piece of paper indicating the extent of their trust to the point of *"what's mine is not yours."*

Now, I ask you: *what's wrong with that picture?* How can trust that grew so strong over time end up on a piece of paper? For one, there is no complete surrender in that trust because there is still reason for concern or distrust.

Although in this modern day and age such a piece of paper can create more piece of mind, I am merely sketching this scenario as food for thought.

Trust is a powerful ability of man to either make or break his integrity. We unfortunately cannot go about and make each potential partner sign on the dotted line to ensure that our safety zone is not violated. We resort to the old traditional ways of "word of bond"-we trust what the person says is true and just as testimony to their character.

The word Trust is an actual abreviation of a deeper meaning of great importance:

Total
Relinquishment of
Unconditional
Sublime
Truth

If you feel this word means anything other than the above statement, please feel free to dissect it in its totality into whatever you wish it to be in application to your situation or viewpoint in life.

CHAPTER 3

"Repairing Shattered Trust"

"Repairing Shattered Trust"

Walk into your local pharmacy and you can get medication for any ailment. The question to all this is how does one find a remedy for the conditions of an aching soul?

Many people have different remedies...from seeing a psychiatrist, speaking to a religious leader, or finding the answer in a highly recommended book. Although all those suggestions might give some kind of closure and answer, none of them can completely heal the pain inflicted.

If the betrayal of trust came from a person of no importance in our lives, it is like water rolling off the back of a duck. The pain and feeling that lingers will remain firm if this act of sabotage came from a spouse, partner, friend, or any person where trust was given to.

Let's see to how to survive or deal with shattered trust.

When our trust is betrayed, we need to take stock of the damage done and do a current evaluation of the importance of the relationship. This can be related to someone being burglarized; nothing can be done about the goods stolen or damage done. Only a report can be filed with the insurance agency, and the police contacted to further follow-up the aftermath of bringing the culprits to justice. Irrespective of what happens, life needs to go on. Now, let's put this synergy into role-play.

When we enter into a relationship, the foremost concern is trust. We give our partners the benefit of the doubt to uphold that oath by surrendering and entrusting our all to them, be it physical, financial, spiritual, or emotional.

Once this betrayal act has happened, we feel robbed of something of great value. We feel hurt, violated, and helpless. The difference in this regard in respect to being burglarized is we know who the culprit is, mystery solved. Now, dealing with this can be complicated.

The following suggestion can be taken:

a.   <u>Stay Composed:</u> Regardless of the severity of the act, remain composed by staying focused on the subject at hand. Allow yourself to stay centered in the moment by requesting an hour or a day to deal with the impact. You were at the receiving end so you determine the time-out period. Use that time to remain free by crying or going for a very long walk. Many people do different things to deal with such emotions.

b.   <u>Acceptance:</u> No one has to accept anything other than by choice-but regardless of how much you hoped and wished that your partner did not betray your trust, accept that it happened and realize there is nothing you can do to reverse or undo it. One might think back to "what could I have done?" The fact remains that you already did all you could do by trusting. Accept your emotion of betrayal and understand that this is the first step to recovery.

c.   <u>Evaluate:</u> Now that you have remained composed as to what has happened and accepted the facts, react with a clear and unclouded mind, for your unleashed hostility clouded by emotion can only lead to further conflict, pain, and anguish. Look at the facts at hand that led up to this unfortunate event. You might be surprised to find who started the snowball effect. However, this is no excuse for betrayal. Chart all the important facts down on paper, similar to a court reporter. Call your partner and set up a meeting to discuss the events and solution or conclusion to the relationship.

d. <u>Open Floor:</u> Ask your partner to elaborate on the events that led up to the betrayal. Don't believe them when the words "I Love You" mysteriously appear, it might be a ploy to soften the already hardened blow. The question is where was that LOVE when the act occurred? Whether the act was through infidelity or trusted confidential information revealed to parties not concerned in the relationship, it does not matter…there's no small trust and big trust…Trust is Trust.

e. <u>Closure</u>: Now is the time when choices need to be made after the facts were revealed. You can either trust again and risk it happening again, or end the relationship, for it is only a matter of time until you realize your feelings have changed towards the person you entrusted your heart and soul to. Be as it may, the choice will remain yours. Find closure to your emotions so you can move on freely to the life you feel you deserve.

f. <u>The Love that causes the Boomerang Affect</u>: After all is said and done, make sure of one thing: that you are honest and truthful towards yourself. Do not be plagued by the guilt of having made a choice, whether it was for the better or worse. Do not heed too much the advice or input of your friends or family; it might lead you further astray. The choice is yours and yours alone to make. If you choose to make that mistake again by returning to that relationship…it's okay. Our own experiences and mistakes will make up our understanding of a condition. Some people become "Boomerangs"-forgiving consistently and going back to the relationship of deceit and pain.

The mentality of some individuals is:

a. I can do it, he/she loves me so much that they will forgive me and keep coming back, because they know what I offer.

b. I have a perfect relationship and can get away with anything to give me a thrill.

c. I like variety, she/he has to get use to it or leave....I don't care.

d. Whatever I do...I cover my tracks too well for it to come out, so I will chance it.

The list goes on and on, but you must remember...Life Goes On.

The sad thing in this regard is that this betrayal might damage our belief in society or in people as a whole. This condition might cause us to throw away that precious Trust that can be treasured and appreciated by a total stranger that truly deserves it.

So, give life a chance by realizing that everyone is different and will not do to you what your partner has done. Have faith that there is good in people and trust in another.

Long after the deed was done, you need to know that a scar will remain. Make sure that it is hidden discreetly yet seen by all. Many do not understand this statement, so let me explain. You do not have to be cruel and bitter towards other people to prove how much you were hurt. Keep your humanity and sincerity in mind. Your scars need to be visible in such a way that you are truthful with the next person about your experiences. Once they know up front how much you were hurt through betrayal, they will tread carefully.

As a point of advice, ask that potential partner if they have ever betrayed a loved one's trust and to what extent. That will give you an immediate picture of who and what you are dealing with.

Golden Rule:

Try not to make the same mistake twice.

CHAPTER 4

"The Price of Truth"

"The Price of Truth"

"The truth will set you free"…well so they say. My question is: are you prepared to pay the ultimate price for truth's sake?

Truth is a powerful element of bright light that incases itself in the words of fact. It can cut to the deepest region of a fragile or able soul, breaking free from the darkness of confusion and lies.

Since an early age we were taught by our parents or guardian to speak the truth, for therein is the ability to be a respectable and trustworthy person. Our trustworthiness and ability to tell the truth can measure the character of one's existence. Lies can be described as obscuring the authentic version of a factual event, comment, or matter.

Every one of us has told a fib one way or the other to protect someone or exaggerate the truth to give substance to the subject or topic of discussion. To lie is a factual condition within us all to preserve the persona of our individuality. No one can say that they have never lied before. To tell the truth can bring personal shame upon our actions that we hoped would remain unnoticed or undiscovered.

The suggestion, however, is that we must try our best to live honorably, by telling the truth and remaining a trusted individual within our own perception of being human. The effect truth has on the psyche of humans can be relieving or disasterous, so be cautious when speaking it.

Here are a few things to consider before you decide to be the Hero or Savior of the moment to tell the whole Truth and nothing but:

Example 1: A friend or stranger sits next to you. During conversation, you detect that their breath gives off an unpleasant odor. How would you react for the sake of truth?

Suggestions before you answer:

a. Evaluate and Analyze: During your conversation, determine if the individual can deal with a direct comment or truthful approach by reading their mood state or character. Not everybody can handle the truth as you might speculate. Remember the golden rule…do unto others as you would like done to you.

b. Power of Suggestion: There are various ways of suggesting a resolution. If you do not have a mint in your bag or pocket, then don't even consider mentioning it. Your actions might be viewed as inconsiderate. If you do have a mint, take one…enjoy it and place it back in your pocket. A minute or what later, apologize for your inconsideration and offer them a helping. If they choose to refuse, then it's their choice. If they accept then they might be thinking the following. "Thank goodness…I needed that!!" or "Is he/she trying to say something…and if he/she is…how courteous to go about it in that manner!"

Overview: Evaluate the situation, analyze the need to respond appropriately, have the Power of Suggestion of self-application, and be courteous in approach before the Truth is said.

Example 2: You see your best friend's partner kissing and hugging another at a remote location. Do you contact them and reveal this traitorous act or remain silent?

If you answered "contact them", the following could happen because of you not following the basic guide to consideration before revealing the truth.

*You told your friend, he/she over-reacted, kicked the partner to the curb...and everything went wrong. Weeks later you find out the person was a long-lost cousin of 12 years and they met each other at the most awkward place. Before he/she could tell the partner of that day's event, you jumped the gun. All hopes of happiness were destroyed because of your impulse to tell the truth.

Truth is just two letters away from the words Trust...so they walk hand in hand. It is best to understand your situation before you consider being the truthful hero.

Whether going for a job interview or meeting that potential mate, it is important to reveal the truth of your past dealings pertaining to the subject at hand. I am not saying to tell of all you have done in the past, only to assure the individual of your trustworthiness. If you are hiding something that could be an important determining factor for the future relation, it is best to speak of it. When posed with uncomfortable questions, make your reasons clear so as not to cast a shadow of doubt over the credibility of your words.

One's past is an unchangable condition, yet it is of great relevance to determine the future outcome of a situation. It is not right to be judged upon our past, yet it is a crucial piece in the jigsaw puzzle of life. Our past needs to be accepted by society and, foremost, by ourselves.

Do not dwell on the circumstances of the past, but show compassion and remorse for wrongful acts to free oneself from the chains of pity, remorse, regret, and shame.

We all want to be free from past errors with no trace of wrongdoing, but that is impossible. Many people who have not faltered in life tend to come across as truthful beings with high standards, morals, and ethics that society deems fit and exemplary. That will only last as long as the day you tell a lie to cover for a friend, or lie to set yourself free from the blame and effects of an action.

The psychological reason for telling the truth is to free our conscious mind of concern, fear, retribution, and blame from an action or word uttered. This condition is known as having a "Clear Conscience".

Truth is a profound substance within man that can set him free or imprison his mind until TIME comes along and reveals all. This substance of truth is a direct reflection of our character and inner being. If it is in our nature to be truthful, our words and deeds will walk along each other in harmony and respect for all to see.

If one lies…the Truth will eventually come out in our nature of character determined by our circumstances.

We lie to our partners and family because of personal shame or because we do not want to hurt their feelings. We lie on our credit application because we need the money urgently. We lie at a job interview so we can get the job for whatever reason. We lie to the IRS so we can keep that little bit of extra we got. We lie to the law in fear of a stiff sentence or punishment. We lie to each other because it's all about who looks better in the eyes of society. We lie about our past because we fear rejection. We lie about our credentials because we want to be viewed as successful individuals, and not misfits of life.

Why do we do it? Is it in our nature, humanity, or just because society determined it so to survive and be noted?

The price of truth is sometimes high, because we loose that potential mate, lucrative deal, ideal job, our character of credibility and foremost...our humanity.

A prisoner of war will endure the torture and anguish of pain and suffering by lying to protect the Truth. To tell the truth to the enemy can be viewed as an easy escape from prosecution or suffering, thus labeling them as being a weakling, subordinate, and dishonourable, bringing shame upon the country and its people. Not all can endure a moral choice based upon the adversity of the moment. For the POW, the anticipation of death is worse than death itself.

Many will pass their judgment and say they would have done otherwise, yet when exposed to those conditions...the tables will turn.

To tell the Truth is a moral choice we all will make one time or another, but it is as certain as death and taxes.

Truth+Trust=Honorable Character of Strength in Word and Deed.

CHAPTER 5

"When is Enough, Enough!!"

"When is Enough, Enough!!"

There comes a time in any relationship when one feels "to this point and no further". We all know our own limitations to enduring an emotion.

Overloading anything with a maximum weight capacity can result in inevitable disaster. If the equation in this example is logic, then why is it so difficult for people to understand their own limitations?

We tend to compromise too much with overbearing circumstances. If you had $2.50 to travel from New Jersey to New York, would you still attempt the journey knowing you had a financial prolem? Surely not...so the moral of this example is that we know prior to departure on a relationship how far we will be able to travel with the cash or tolerance at hand.

Everyone has a different tolerance level in different circumstances. You might endure the harsh words of your employer daily, but will snap the moment your partner gives you that unkind glance. During the initial phase of a relationship we find out much about our partners, from what they like to what they want to become. One of the most important factors that need to be remembered in this regard is the tolerance level, or their PTL. In my terms, Patience Tolerance Level.

If your partner has a "short fuse", as the cowboys would say, you are in a heap of trouble if you think you can say or do the same uncalled deed more than once. From that standpoint you can clearly determine the inevitable outcome of the relationship if something happens more than what it's supposed to. Embrace yourself for a lifetime of making up if that line is crossed more than needed.

Sometimes the love we feel for our partners creates a "That's Okay Zone", that allows them to repeat that hurtful act over and over. As long as you steer away from your initial belief in what your PTL told you from the word "GO", the more you must understand that you will become a victim of your own demise. Strangely enough, your friends will be the ones who will notice the pattern with the famous "I told you so" punch line.

Your endurance level must be a vital component to the sphere of the relationship. Make your likes and dislikes openly known prior to persuing a relationship. If you are past that point before realising it, then let me help in resetting your PTL meter, pronto, before you become a walking time-bomb.

Resetting you PTL Meter:

a. Take stock of your current situation by just writing down your dislikes in your relationship. They will guide you to the core of the mountain. Do not write down your concerns, we all have them and the list can become endless…for it ties too closely to insecurities, doubts, and fears. Focus on the task at hand.

b. Number and chart them down in priority order. You might find yourself re-arranging this more than once.

c. Ask your partner to do the same, and decide upon a convenient time to discuss it.

d. After the exchange of dislikes, you discuss what is possible and doable.

e. If a stalemate is reached on one or two of the issues, it is time for compromise.

How to Compromise:

The answer is easy. Stop thinking selfishly, technically, or in a complex manner.

"If the compromise is of mutual benefit for the relationship, then change is good."

If not, re-evaluate your status in the relationship as being part of the problem or part of the solution. You as partners know each other better than any book, shrink, or friend. It all depends on what you share with whom. You do the math.

Many men and women listen...but don't Hear each other...Speak...but don't Talk to each other...Look...but don't See each other.

When your partner speaks to you regarding any subject, stop whatever it is you are doing (although difficult at times), look them in the eyes and take in every word they say. It might be a plea to save something you are not even aware of that needs saving.

Always remember...There is a time and place for everything. Do not expect the abovementioned during a commute, brief road trip, church meeting, movie theatre, or any circumstance that can lead to further problems.

However, if that partner treasures all that you are about, he/she will *make time* and stay true to their word to follow it up. Do not expect them to read your mind and bring concerning matters to attention...nothing beats conversation.

Prevention is better than cure.

CHAPTER 6

"Maturity with Age or Experience?"

"Maturity with Age or Experience?"

This topic can easily turn into a heated debate, and I strongly suggest you use it as a good topic of constructive discussion at the next get-together with your friends.

Does maturity come with age or experience? I will say "Yes!"…either one or neither nor, read this chapter and make the determination for yourself.

If we look at the global village children grow up in, we realize that geographical location, time-zones, foods, social economical structures, and traditional values play a big role in their intellectual perception of things.

I believe in coming of age through mature experiences, but if you wish to be direct and to the point I will say maturity comes with experience, and this is why I feel so strongly about it:

For many years I thought that the older you get, the wiser and mature you become. I realized that the only thing that does mature is your physical frame of body through the natural process of growth. I became further confused when I watched the TV family dramas. Webster, Doogie Howser, and Different Strokes, all with boy geniusus. Athough fictional dramas, they were a realistic reflection of what happens in the real world.

What was it that made us mature? To find the answer I drew my conclusions from my own experiences and those of people I know. If a child is exposed to harsh conditions of labor, survival, and struggles of the adult world, they mature unnaturally before their time. It is almost a sin again Mother Nature to make a child experience that which an adult endures. Just because a child does what the adults do does not create wisdom in maturity.

That condition comes from the ability to intellectually make individual sound choices based upon logic and reason.

Our maturity lies within the experiences we encounter as a child or adult. Today there are many people in their 30's or even 40s'-50s' that act more childish than some teens. We might say it is a young soul caught in an old body, and perhaps it is so. The spirit or zest for life might be there, but the physical body might not keep up.

It is not always important for the spirit and body to be in accord. Realize that all that is happening to our bodies through aging is simply turning back into an infant. We become as helpless and dependable on care as babies do. All we have to show after all the years is the penny of wisdom and experiences, along with an energetic spark for the life we cling onto.

Our maturity makes up our enduring lessons learned in life, as well as applying them to our everyday life.

The maturity of intimacy:

The norm is that sexuality is directed towards the maturer sector in society, based upon the age factor. Yet somehow the younger generation got caught up in this race for adulthood by engagement in sexual conduct.

The moment a teenager partakes in this act, they seemingly forget the immense responsibility that comes with it, be it disease or pregnancy. Even more disturbing is that these facts are the breakdown of values that make each individual respect themselves. This hip and newfounded bliss of experience can only be traced back to the family structure of maturity.

The act of mature intimacy used to be reserved for the couples with an age intellect and adult understanding, believing in the commitment of exclusivity.

One of the most important factors that makes up the maturity of this act actually happens long before intimacy takes place. It is called "becoming friends for life". Maturity in a relationship normally follows the following criteria, which some of you might respond to by saying "Yeah in a perfect world!", but all it takes is personal preference and not criteria set by society.

The patient and mature approach to a relationship:

a. You meet someone you like, due to similar interest or belief.

b. You go on several dates as friends, respecting each others' freedom as individuals.

c. After several months or years you introduce your partner to your family and circle of comfort.

d. During all this there is a mutual consent on intimacy based upon commitment.

e. Talk of further commitment is on the table and inevitably leads to marriage.

The quick-fix of the modern relationship:

a. You meet someone you like, mutual or not.

b. You are in hot persuit of that person for the sake of finding intimacy or personal gain.

c.   The act of intimacy happens, feelings are hurt, and relationships destroyed.

d.   Moving on to the next person where the same thrill can be found.

And the bottom line is? None of the above methods can guarantee happiness or eternal bliss. The determining factor to that success and happiness lies in the mutual goals of the partners over a long period of time. I'm not going to get involved in the debate "Sex before Marriage"…hmmm…well, I can't resist, so let me voice my opinion in this regard.

Sex is a mature act of consent between two adults. The possible consequences of it can lead to pregnancy or marriage by circumstances or mutual interest.

If you are not prepared to accept the consequences of your actions and what it may lead to…LEAVE IT ALONE!!!!!!…you can destroy the most promising of careers or hopeful aspirations of an individual.

I am not going to take it any further than this. I feel this explanation is direct and to the point. Oh! That will be another constructive topic of discussion at your next get-together. You might as well keep a pen and paper handy, for I will be dropping various hints as to what to debate.

CHAPTER 7

"Crowded Room, Lonely Place"

"Crowded Room, Lonely Place"

Is it not funny how one can feel extremely lonely in a crowded room?

I truly believe that every human being is a significant planet with abundant life and is an integral part of the cosmic spectrum in the universe. We are all somehow linked together through the fiber of life and existence, believe it or not.

No one wants to be alone, and I do not mean it in the sense of a human relationship. Some of us choose to spend our days with a loving pet or anything that drives our passion for life and fills those empty spaces of time. There is nothing wrong with that, after all, it's our personal preference to do so.

What makes a Homosapien relationship unique is the trial, tribulation, or happiness it brings. Pets will never deny your need for attention; they give freely with no obligation and sometimes give their lives in return. Perhaps we can learn something from them. However, to be honest…dealing with pets and everything else is an easy way out of making your life complicated due to a partner. The rewards of a relationship does wonders for the soul when the right person is found. I do not mean the right person as in Mr. or Miss Right, but that one who tickles our fancy or with whom we have a mutual understanding to last for a considerable amount of time.

To be lonely is more devastating than being alone. How? You go to work alone, do what you like, practically…if you are not handicapped, no disrespect intended, you would do everything by yourself.

Loneliness is an empty feeling of loss and isolation that eats on the insides of your mind, second by second, minute by minute, day after day. If we do not have a sense of belonging to someone or something, we become lost in the river of time and fear the fateful ending of dying alone and without anyone having known of our existence.

The question is what to do about that loneliness. Fill it with something you have a passion for and realize you need to be contented with your situation in accepting yourself and your conditions. Remember that no condition will last forever, it will come and go. Do not err in life by making haste to experience that sense of belonging. You are better off with what is comfortable than dealing with adverse changes you are not prepared for.

We are all different in various social settings; thus we are different in dealing with various conditions in life. The keyword to your contentment is Acceptance. Many people become lonely because they refuse to accept the fact that they need to be alone.

One of the biggest problems we have when on the social scene is that we treat each new encounter with the possible expectation of a romantic rendezvous. Our expectation should be in the pursuit of friends. The anticipation of something potential could end in sure disaster due to the diversity in personal preference across a broad spectrum. Do not expect too much of the opposite gender at first glance or encounter. The best of friends makes the best of lovers...for they know and understand your every thought. Yet, that line is very fine and should not be risked for the pursuit of happiness and dissapation of loneliness.

Be sure not to mistake your loneliness for individuality. Some people cannot distinguish between the two and tend to sacrifice their individuality as a human being to accommodate that feeling of belonging.

At every event you will find that clown that is the center of attraction, either through his/her humor or acting the fool to breathe life into a dull event. That might be their way of dealing with the inevitable loneliness when they return home. Sometimes a happy exterior shows an unhappy interior. Things are not always what they seem, however, so tread carefully before you assume someone is lonely. They might just be contented.

CHAPTER 8

"Engagement & Marriage"

"Engagement & Marriage"

All roads in most serious relationships lead to the commitment of engagement or marriage.

One word comes to mind when I see those two words: "exclusivity", or in layman's terms, "Off Limits" to the opposite sex. Although engagement is but one step closer to the act of marriage, the commitment to it should be a reflection thereof.

Many people tend to stray even though they are engaged to be married...Why? Simple, it is either in their nature, it is fear of being out of the single scene, fear of being with the same person for the rest of your life, or there are unresolved matters that are not being taken seriously.

There are various forms of engagement:

a. Mutual Engagement:

This is an exciting period in the couple's lives when they decide to take it to the next level after a number of years. The emphasis is on "mutual", so it immediately tells you the two worked towards a common goal knowingly, willingly, and freely. They both have an in-depth understanding of each other's world and how to merge the two. The love that binds this choice can and will last for a very long time...or for as long as they want it to last.

b. Obligatory Engagement:

After a 6 or 7 year period or longer, the partner wonders when they will be asked to get married. The time as they feel is right financially, socially, and emotionally...well so they hope. If there was no talk of further commitment after the first 4 years, then there is need to review where the relationship is going. Eventually after much pressure and obligation to do the right thing, you get engaged. The strong "want" will be so strong from the one partner that the other decides to do it in good faith. How long do you think this relationship, married or not, will last when the first bump in the road arises? The unwilling partner might slowly but surely place obstacles in the road for the other to notice that it was not a mutual and free choice.

c.   <u>Eggs in one Basket Engagement:</u>

This kind of event can happen whether the social or financial conditions are right or not. This method goes against the logic and reason of action, and very often is condemned by society. The driving force in this is "passion and love"-the instinctive impulse to take a big step without considering the repucussions or consequences of our actions. That kind of action sometimes leads to happiness not found in many relationships. Risky but rare. Las Vegas can testify to this.

d.   <u>Contractual Engagement:</u>

This is what it sounds like. Black on white in ink and paper. Some couples decide to join their wealth and status in society, thus making it seem the most perfect and convenient relationship. As some rules are meant to be broken, so does contractual engagement. If both parties feel that the contract has outlived its purpose, they tend to close shop in search for the next ride offering them a swift journey to further recognition, fame, and fortune.

Marriage:

Matters concerning marriage can be placed under the same unbrella; the only difference is the commitment aspect of exclusivity. Many fear marriage like the plague, and will do their best to avoid it. An engagement can be broken or delayed, but a marriage is a set event that can not just be cancelled like a cable channel. Once you are married…you are married. I am not saying to take engagement lightly, but realise that it does not guarantee happiness for the rest of your life and it can be altered at will of choice.

The engagement period needs to be used to iron out all the wrinkles in the relationship. Do not perceive to fix it once you are married. It will be do or die, and you do not want to be there. Many times you know what damage a certain concern can have once you are married, but you choose to ignore it, being too wrapped up in the hustle and bustle of wedding planning and emotional bliss of the big day.

The ideal thing to do is to sit down with your partner and speak of all concerns, from finances to living and loving. You need to know the mind frame of eternal commitment from your partner before you decide to pull out all the stops and plan a wedding fit for a king and queen.

Wedding jitters can cause a beautiful thing to turn into a nightmare of fear, concern, and doubt. Deal with your insecurities and concerns long before you decide to take that leap of faith in another.

Marriage is not child play and should be done in good faith and sanctity of consideration and willingness to walk that road to the very end. And after all this, happiness and eternal bliss is not guaranteed. Reaching that height is easier than staying there. Know yourself, know your partner, know your circumstances, and you are well on your way to finding that contentment in the happiness of marriage.

There are many books that tell you of this commitment, but I have cut to the chase. Do not over-analyze or read too many books. Reading about it is often different than living it and dealing with a partner. Just learn to know yourself and know what makes you happy before taking that step.

CHAPTER 9

"Infidelity"

"Infidelity"

Now, where do I start regarding this subject of discussion? I bet there are many who skipped all other chapters and jumped right to this one. This sensitive subject will touch many heartstrings of those who can relate and those who acted accordingly.

Why do people cheat? And what does it actually entail?

Before we can venture further on this topic, know this…everyone at one point or another has done it. The question is to what extent. One can do so in thought, in spirit, and in the act of physical engagement. When does it qualify as infidelity? I believe it to be so when the partner knowingly acts upon the impulse of lust, passion or emotion with someone other than their mate. This act leads to the betrayal of trust I spoke of in earlier chapters.

The painful realization that one's partner has committed this act leaves an unforgettable scar that can haunt the happiest of relationships to the bitter end. That betrayal often leads to retaliation with a similar act, or simply the breakdown of the relationship.

One of the contributing factors in both genders that leads to this is availability, variety, and challenge. Even though their partner offers all the abovementioned, there is a primal instinct that is written in the genetic code of mankind to hunt and women to gather. Too many use that as an excuse and these days it is just not acceptable. We have evolved way past that primal heritage into a civilized culture of choices and consideration.

The various forms of Infidelity:

a) Conceptual Infidelity:

Both partners are aware of each other's desire to be with another, to have the best of both worlds, and yet have a solid foundation or understanding.

b) Justified Infidelity:

Once the partner discovers they were cheated on, they will knowingly do likewise in order to soften the blow and get back at their partner in an eye for an eye and tooth for a tooth scenario.

c) Knowing Infidelity:

This act happens when the partner knows the commitment and inevitable response of their partner or spouse and then risk it knowingly to add spice to life for no reason. All for the sake of adventure.

Irrespective of the reason for this act, it was, is, and never will be right. This action can cause an individual on the receiving end to loose their self-esteem, commitment, love, happiness, and zest for life. Depression normally follows directly thereafter. To deal with this dilemma, refer to the chapter dealing with how to repair shattered trust and the price of truth.

As long as one engages in this act and returns to the comforts of the trusting relationship, it will always be wrong. During a seperation stage where both parties know that there will be no return to the sanctity of a marriage or relationship, this act cannot be called cheating. It only applies to the betrayal of a committed relationship where trust is invested and both live in a mutual acceptance of exclusivity. If you feel otherwise...please feel free to add this to your notes on "topic of discussions". If a man or woman chooses to be with someone else, knowing that they have irreconcilable differences with their partners that led to a seperation or divorce, that act needs to be carefully reviewed within the stigma of commitment.

We all feel differently in this regard and it is justifiably so. Regardless if the relationship is platonic or dually committed, infidelity stings the same and leaves the person feeling used, worthless, cheap, unappreciated, hurt, unhappy, and tormented. The only way to truly recover from it is to evaluate your true emotion and have what you will, whether it is leaving the relationship or mending the wounds of infliction. It is your choice.

Do not destroy the spirit of another for the sake of lust or a cheap thrill of the moment. Place yourself in the shoes of the one who is about to discover the treacherous act. If you wish not to inflict pain to yourself, do not do it to another, for the day will come when what you have done to another will be done to you.

CHAPTER 10

"Manipulation"

"Manipulation"

Manipulation is the psychological ability to modify a situation for one's own benefit through the alteration of facts, circumstances, or emotions.

We all have encountered this in a relationship. If you have not, then perhaps it is because the manipulator is not so obvious as to be detected. Trust me, if you are thinking about it, it already happened.

This form of emotional mind game is very innocent at first glance, but potentially dangerous in the long haul. The predecessor that gives rise to manupulation is called "Guilt Trip", which plays on your ability to have compassion for a situation and exploiting it. I can see how many are nodding in recognition. Now "guilt trip" has a little critter working on the job called "finding and knowing your weakness", and they all work for the crime boss "Cunningness". There is so much influence at the end of the day that you have no other choice but to overturn your individual choice in a matter from yes to no or vice-versa.

If you sit back and watch this interesting group at work, you will be surprised at the human ability to discover new ways to outwit or alter a situation for self-interest.

Here is a classical example:

You walk into the store and your partner sees an item with a costly price tag. (No! I am not referring to woman or a man, it can be either of the two.) They know you will only buy out of necessity, and not luxury. So they approach you and take out the invisible bag of past transgressions. You now need to pay for past mistakes…literally. If you do not, you know they will walk around with that notion of what you did, thus putting "guilt trip" at the forefront, minipulation in the flank, and cunning in the background. Once these three do their job, boy! Oh boy!...do you see them go...

Now that they have control over the situation, it is guaranteed that you will walk out of that store with a bitter taste on the pallet.

It is guaranteed that your partner will not forget that encounter, and it is almost sure that they will try and find a way to get back at you. If that, however, is not in their nature or character, you will have lost a piece of yourself. If it continues, be sure to end up single before the relationship's expiration date.

You might get away with it the first few times, but there will come a time when all you will be left is the gain of your endeavor and the loss of a wonderful partner. Is it worth the risk? We need to respect each other's individual right to refuse or say "No" to something we are not happy with. If that right is taken away, we violate the most basic respect and mutual appreciation in the relationship.

Being flirtatious with manipulation can be fun and filled with innocent intentions. Some get so much gratification from the result that they become scholars in this art. They inevitably achieve a Master's Degree, leaving behind a path of destruction, betrayal, and hurt, a price too costly in terms of emotion.

You do the emotional crime...you will do the emotional time, in the dog house or prison of loneliness.

CHAPTER 11

"The First Bond of the Intimicy Law"

"The First Bond of the Intimicy Law"

Wonder what this chapter is all about? Well, this has everything to do with the law that binds a soul to another through the act of intimacy the first time. In other words, loosing one's virginity. Many do not realise the implication of this act and the reasons for feeling a certain way afterwards. I will attempt to give some clarity. Although a man, I will view this through the eyes of a woman and fellow human being with emotions and consideration.

This subject needs to be given the utmost respect and needs to be read over and over until you can grasp this concept and its importance. I will be brief and to the point.

This law does not apply to men as extensively as with women. Why? Women are intellectual beings with an in-depth psyche of emotions that tops the highest mountain and surveys the lowest valley, with the most complex approach imaginable.

Women are taught at an early age to reserve their womanhood for the right person-being their husbands-why? What they have is something special and unique that spiritualy binds them to their husbands and I call it the Bond of the Law.

Regardless of how the spouse or the partner treats her, whether it is physical abuse or cheating, she will feel a compelling connection to unwillingly remain in the relationship, dedicating her life to staying at his side. Many say it is for the sake of the marriage or relationship, but trust me it is not. Such a bond is very difficuilt to break away from, even if turned sour.

Today's teenagers do not consider this fact. I am extending a word of sincere caution to all those who value the importance of that gift. Give it to someone you intend spending the rest of your life with. Do not throw it away for the sake of a cheap thrill or peer pressure. The older you get the more you realise the truth in this matter.

Then again…nothing guarantees you happiness or bliss in a relationship. Just make sure you are not sweet-talked into becoming just another notch on someone's belt.

Just a word of note: Men experience a sensation and gain something thrilling to talk about tomorrow. Women loose something precious and remain bound to it.

CHAPTER 12

"Breakups & Divorces"

"*Breakups & Divorces*"

Whether the relationship is platonic or true, breaking up is never an easy thing. Some teens and adults go to extremes to avoid this inevitable phase in a dissipating relationship, resulting in more emotional torment than bargained for.

No relationship ends abruptly. It is a gradual ending of something happy or potential for a long-term success. Some relations can turn sour after a few weeks, months, or even many years, but it does happen. Anyone who is engaged in a relationship either fears or knows that step that awaits around every explosive argument or event to joepardize the calm existence of life.

The moment something goes wrong or there is reason for concern we think about the ending outcome. Do we brace for impact or do we pay heed to the warning signs?

No one is free from this potential painful and disappointing emotion. We break up from our partners or spouse because there is no trust, faith, hope, or love left.

Most contibuting factors leading to this I have already discussed in all previous chapters. If you skipped them and dove right to this one, then I suggest you take the long and safe route and read them. Do not read this for a quick fix, for it ties in with all proceeding chapters.

You must realise that breaking up or inevitably getting a divorce are not the only options to dealing with the turbulent existance of a relationship. That step can somehow be seen as the humanitarian way to end pain, anguish, unhappiness, and lack of affection, before the fiber of self-worth is completely destroyed.

Ending a relationship does not guarantee the emotional resolution. Even if one person pursues another relationship, the mind holds the memories of past experiences and unhappiness.

Now that you have a brief overview, let me discuss in-depth how to avoid or deal with the occurance of breakup and the aftermath.

Breaking-Up:

This situation happens to couples who are not committed to the point of marriage. The emotional distress caused by this might be severe, but the financial and circumstantial implications could be worse during a divorce.

The tell-tale signs of an inevitable break-up show weeks, months, or even years later, normally happening within the first, second, or third in-depth conversation you have with your potential partner. How?...follow the pawprints into the rabbit's hole.

Early Warning Signs:

During early courtship, you discuss all the basic issues like hobbies, likes, dislikes, movies, other interests, religious and political beliefs. It is advisable to ask that potential partner their viewpoint regarding commitment, long term goals regarding a relationship, hopes, dreams, and aspirations. Compare them to what it is you want and make the determination if you two would end up happy and contented, or just barely surviving by the strings of mercy.

Example: If your potential partner says that they never want kids and furnish their reasons, and you are feeling otherwise...the warning bells need to go off and alert your senses of this coming dilemma. Do not say "Ah! Well he/she will change their mind" and then a few years later you bring the subject up and expect them to have a sudden change of heart.

One's dreams, hopes, and aspirations cause us to seek that one who would fullfill that requirement...if they do not...and they are willing to compromise and change...then regard yourself as fortunate.

All I am saying and strongly emphasize on...prevention is better than cure!

Dealing with a Break-up:

When that inevitable bombshell is dropped on you, demand that it be done face to face, the same way it started. Therein lies the courtesy and mutual respect for each other. If that person wishes not to do it, trust me that they will always duck and dive to avoid the music. It takes courage and confidence to approach a person and start a conversation, and so it is to end a relationship.

Your future concept of relationships will largely depend on how your previous one ended. Animosity can be a bitter substance that poisons the soul and creates suffering. No one wants to be dumped or left for whatever reason. Just remember and understand that every individual has a free and willing choice in everything they do. Do not mope around saying you were dumped. In doing so you create a negative force of self-pity and break down your confidence in that which you are as a person.

If you were left for some invalid reason and weak excuse that will not hold up in your books, then search deeper till you find proper closure to the situation. Just demand honesty and truth so you can be set free from nagging question of "Why?" If that person was the only one in the world for you, then it would be proper to say "Houston! We have a problem!"...whereas if you look about today, there are others. Do not seclude yourself from the world and pledge a vow of celibacy for the sake of what another has done. Your dignity as a person needs to be treasured by you and carried in high regard. Do not expect another to do it for you. If you knock your toe on the sidewalk, no one is going to stop and rub it for you, but you alone.

The sun still rises and sets and so your life needs to go on. You know what kind of person you are and what you attract. Strive to be who you are as a human being with compassion, honesty, and dignity with respect for others. If you feel used, know that whoever did that to you will get their reward from the Circle of Cause and Effect.

Divorce:

There are so many books on this subject. When you hear the word divorce, you immediately relate to it by your own experience or by knowing of someone close who is about to do it or has endured it.

Divorce was, is, and will always be a painful and an unpleasant facet of the human learning curve, and I can very much relate to it. There is great concern for the increase in divorces. I think a crucial contributing factor is the duration in courtship in preparation for that step of marriage. Another fateful mistake is turning a blind eye on detrimental facts prior to marriage. We end up in an hourglass relationship, slowly but surely running out of time.

The intersting factor is that there is so much hatred, anguish, sorrow, pain, and suffering before the final divorce papers indicate "dissolved", but when the storm subsides, you will find yourself understanding and getting along with that ex either much better or worse than before.

Now the question remains: "was that extreme condition necessary to bring about understanding?" For some the answer is "yes" and for others it is "no".

There is no use in crying over spilled milk; once those papers are signed…they are signed. That does not mean your life is totally over with that person. If there are children, the scenario changes. Being a piece of paper or not, there will be always something linking you to that ex, insignificant or not… and it is that you once were married and shared a life with them.

Some of the ugliest divorces started out as a fairytale of bliss and happiness. I do not need to tell you what went wrong. If you have read all the chapters, you know who said or did what to whom to lead up to it.

Look how peoples' faces change if you tell them you are divorced. The very first thing they think is "I wonder what happened and who did what". There are two sides to a story but always one person who pulled the trigger to finally end it all.

People on the singles scene are very cautious of divorcees. Strange how they reject a divorcee who at least knows something about commitment, and accept the "player" who uses and toys with peoples' emotions. But let me tell you this, we have the experience to go in hand with what we want next time round. The single ones still need to walk that path, and 74% of the time they are scared to get married.

Do not judge a divorcee if you have not walked a mile in their shoes. Hope and pray you remain squeaky clean.

The only way you will actually know if that potential divorced partner is something to be considered is if the truth is known as to who caused the marriage to break up leading to a divorce. If your partner had to get a divorce because of his/her infidelity, warning bells! And I will say no more on this subject.

If you are searching for answers in how to deal with a divorce or any other adverse condition of the soul, read my next book. There are various ways when responding to different situations in life, but there is only one way of solving all those ailments of the mind. That is to strengthen the "Self" by rising above the adversities and finding a new and improved "you" through the cultivation of the mind. Believe in your human ability to survive and become a success based upon your lessons learned and battles fought.

CHAPTER 13

"A Time to Heal or Move on."

"A Time to Heal or Move on."

Everyone needs some time-off after a sudden illness or ailment that incapacitates the body. What remedy does the soul need after a traumatic divorce or breakup? Many take some time-out and converge in all kinds of activities to keep their mind occupied. Although that might not be the recommended suggestion, it is surely a start for some on the road to recovery.

A wound heals by degrees, and so do all things in life. The question is how long does it take for one to heal. Healing varies from person to person and depends on how susceptible the individual is to change, as well as the ability to find the strength to move on and open that new chapter in their lives. Be as it may, society sometimes expects one to take years to heal.

The severity of the damage inflicted greatly determines how long the recovery period will last. This might not always be the case. If you understand yourself and have found your strength as an individual to overcome the worst of adversity through past experiences, then you are more fortunate than most to be able to wipe the dust off yourself after you have fallen, then rise and walk onwards.

The judgemental persona of many who do not understand the stregnth or survival capability of a partner or spouse see betrayal in their ability to heal or move on faster. If you look at the circumstances that led up to the inevitable breakup or divorce, you will find the one who opened a new chapter in their lives will be the one who might have been on the receiving end of the anguish inflicted that led to this end.

To carry the anguish of past pain and suffering with you can only increase you chances of becoming unhappy and caged in the prison of the past. Free yourself from what was by learning from past failures. There is no one person that rules all that can say "you will heal or move on when I say so"...that choice lies dorment within every human being until the need arises to react accordingly.

Regardless of how soon we recover or turn over that new leaf in our lives, the memories of what was will always be there within the conciousness of the mind. So in short, your reflections of what happened are but only a thought away from your recovering or falling back into the vivid reminder of the anguish experienced.

If, however, you moved on with your life without having confronted or dealing with the past, you can be guaranteed to be "Scrooged" when you least expect it.

Words of Advice from this Chapter:

1. Resolve the questions and emotions of the past so you can be free to live unhindered tomorrow.

2. Realise that your happiness and memories of the past are only a thought away.

3. Determine by knowing yourself how much time you need to heal before you find resolve to move on.

4. Do not carry anguish, hatred, or remorse around with you; it only adds to your disposition of unhappiness.

5. Embrace the lighter and brighter things in life, such as making new friends and becoming socially active in a group.

6. Try sports or adventure activities that increase your adrenalin level, such as river rafting, bungee jumping, or sky diving.

7. Seek out nature retreats to find the tranquility and calmness that will enhance your life source.

8. Do yoga, aerobics, or spinning with friends.

9. If you have a family, try and get them involved in some of the activities.

10. Spoil yourself by getting a full aromatherapy massage or a retreat to a spa resort.

11. Lastly, pursue that goal you left before it all started, be it completing your education or starting your own business.

Consider your financial situation before pursuing some of the abovementioned activities, although a price can not be placed on restoring the "Self".

CHAPTER 14

"Tools of the trade."

"Tools of the trade."

In order to build a house, one needs various tools to assist in different phases. None of these phases can lead up to the completion of that house without the tools of the trade.

Analysis of a relationship in comparison to a house:

a. Faith=foundation

b. Exclusivity=walls

c. Vision for future goals=windows

d. Trust=Front and Rear doors+keys

e. Intimacy=master bedroom

f. Priorities=other rooms

g. Mutual Activities=Kitchen

h. Personal Space=Bathroom

i. Communication=electrical and plumbing works

j. Love=Roof that covers all.

Tools needed in pursuit of love and companionship:

1. *Confidence:*

    Walking down 14th street, Broadway, Times Square NY, heck…anywhere for that matter, one sees many visually attractive people. Sometimes that beauty can become intimidating to the average "Joe Soap". Are these kinds of people off-limits for the average person? Surely not. Confidence is a strong substance that makes a super-human out of a fragile and insecure individual. Why doesn't Superman become a gym trainer or strong John after his cape is gone? He chooses to become an average reporter with a nerdy persona, unnoticed by the public. Do the math and realize that there is a superhuman in all of us that can do anything.

Do not ever be intimidated by how another looks. The worst that can happen is them saying "No", but it all depends on how you go about it. No one is better than another. Know, believe, and realize it. You are likely to encounter the high and mighty Ms. Prestige or Mr. God's Gift To Women along the way.

2. *Courtesy:*

In this modern day and age, much of the generations have all but lost the old-fashioned ways where men were gentlemen and woman were ladies. Although times have changed, many of the old ways are returning to the social scene, like the trendy fashions of the 70's. These days ladies are looking to be treated with courtesy, and gentlemen appreciated for their considerate efforts. Courtesy is doing something of value and consideration to members of the opposite sex. Before giving a stranger a compliment or open invitation to coffee, be courteous and sincere with no strings attached.

3. *Respect and Sincerity:*

Personal space seems to be the order of the day in a place like New York. If you are not part of a group, club, or circle of friends, you are considered an outsider until you have met certain criteria to become part of that social setting. Before you enter another's "personal bubble", know that it can be anything from exhilarating to adventurous to dangerous. Be prepared to be either met with volatile or subtle rejection to sincere acceptance. Strangely enough, it is the residents not native to New York or whichever city that are approachable and easy to talk to. If you are turned away, respect the receiver's choice to ignore you. Do not be persistent to invade another's space. Use your senses to pick up on subtle messages of like or dislikes.

4. *Understanding:*

Realize that we all come from different backgrounds and social settings, even countries and ethnic groups. What is acceptable in one culture might be taboo in another, so sincere intentions can easily be misunderstood. Take the time to understand your situation, relationship, or partner before you make uncalled jugements that can cause you personal shame.

5. *Humor:*

Life is too short to be taken so seriously. If you choose to go through life without laughter, prepare yourself for a lifetime of bitterness and depression…or take out a membership with Life-Line, for you will be calling there often for support. Laugh at your mistakes and the humour society has to offer. Take that special person to a comedy club or become a comic by entertaining your partner. If you are not so bold, then explore your own funny bones and those of your partner. Laughter is good medicine, but must not be taken out of context. Know when to laugh and smile, for it can provoke awkward moments. There is a time and place for everything. By

knowing anothers comical preference, one can instantly for-
mulate a plan of action for mutual benefit.

6. *Initiative:*

Make life unpredictable by initiating a constructive conversation through open forums amongst friends, partners, or
your spouse. Do not always wait for the other to come up
with new and improved ways to spice up a relationship.
Find out what your partner likes and adores and surprise
them, whether it is a foot massage, dinner and a movie, or
romantic walks. Do not always wait for a special occasion to
hand a gift or flowers. There are so many adventurous things
to do and places to see. Once life becomes monotonous,
make sure that the feeling is mutual between you and the
other party. With the rise of fierce independence, some might
find it offensive if you initiate opening a door or carrying a
book bag, so be sure to ask before initiating an action. The
last thing you want to do is to take your partner to a surprise
"spur of the moment" bungee jumping event, and they
dread heights.

7. *Acceptance:*

We all make mistakes in a relationship, whether it is saying
the wrong thing or doing the inappropriate deed. Learn to
take responsibility for your actions by accepting blame for
the things you knowingly did or uttered by accident. The
sooner you have acceptance to who is at fault, the sooner
tensions will dissipate. It is always easy to claim a prize,
inheritance, or a treasure, but to claim responsibility for a
mistake followed by the consequences of that action
becomes another matter all together. Regardless of the pun-

ishment for the deed, accept that you did wrong by your partner. Learn to accept your situation in the relationship, for you chose to be there. If anything goes wrong with your fantasy world of "love, bliss, and eternal happiness till death do us part", accept the circumstances if you know you have done all you can and looked at acceptance instead of suffering from denial. Do not deny the outcome of a situation if you know you steered the ship to rocky shores. It is always easier to "pass the buck" by blaming it on another. The sooner you accept the unchangeable facts, the sooner you can overcome an obstacle.

8. *Honor:*

Seeing this word, the story of "King Arthur and the Knights of the Round Table" comes to mind. Why? I don't know…I just like the way a knight fought in valor and honor for country, justice, love, or tradition. Honor can be traced to any warrior or soldier in any culture.

To be honorable is to have found a deep-rooted respect in a code of conduct on a path to righteous actions. The way we treat our partners or spouse can determine if there is honor in our intentions. So, who determines what is honorable and not?

Due to the valor that accompanies this word, the code of conduct in a Martial Way, Military Institute, or any system that promotes the character and ethics of an individual to high moral standards, can qualify to set the precedence.

9. *Charitability:*

Although this word makes us think of organizations that assist the needy at no cost, I firmly believe in what my mom used to say: "charity begins at home". I will keep this section in context to relationships. Charity is to give to your partner without expecting anything in return. Although the "give and take" scenario is present in most relations, there is nothing more rewarding than seeing a smile on the face of another because of a deed not expected. I am not saying to empty your wallet or surrender your belongings to your mate, but give in sincerity not expecting anything in return. The hand that gives will always receive. The core of a charitable deed is to not seek recognition for the acts. If you hope for the trumpets to blow and go down in history as a wonderful person, then I strongly recommend that you refrain from doing that charitable task for your partner. How often have you heard this phrase when things go wrong in a relationship: "just remember what I did for you" or "it's because of me you are where you are". Better not to do anything charitable at all.

"Be careful of the Greek Gods bearing gifts". If you don't know what that means, then do some homework and ask around.

*   *   *

Take the time to know your partner long before they become your spouse, and if you are already there, start a new chapter in your life. Better late than never.

CHAPTER 15

"Recipe to Hapiness."

"Recipe to Hapiness."

To make a meal fit for a king or to please the taste buds of the most discerning connoisseurs, one needs to look to a recipe book to prepare such a meal, or turn to a formidable chef.

Many of us turn to our friends and family for advice in how to find that special person, deal with the tribulations of life, or evaluate that potential mate for life. Sometimes books can give a third perspective on such matters.

This recipe might not work for many due to diversity in personality, but it will surely give you an indication of what to have and look for.

A-Z Criteria to Establish long term happiness, leading to marriage or not:

a. Be socially active in large groups to meet people of diversity.

b. Focus on friendship rather than searching for a lover or partner.

c. Find mutual ground regarding long-term goals for the relationship.

d. Respect each other's individual aspirations for success or life.

e. Be financially independent where possible.

f. Support each other in activities pursued before the relationship started.

g. Communicate throughout the relationship by discussing insecurities, fears, and doubts.

h. Be realistic in approach to starting a family.

i. Have mutual respect, trust, and love towards each other.

j. Add spice to life by surprising your partner/spouse.

k. Give flowers just because to make a normal day special.

l. Look at each other when in conversation

m. Discuss the day's events. If there is nothing…find something.

n. Give yourself time-out through personal pampering.

o. Have respect and tolerance for each other's spiritual or religious belief systems.

p. Do some good through charitable work, and do not expect recognition or reward.

q. Do unto your partner as you would like done to you.

r. Accept and learn from mistakes and do not judge one another or others.

s. Be thankful everyday for the small things in life.

t. Find time to go to nature retreats to absorb the energy and tranquillity there.

u. Accept your mortality by tresuring every second and minute by living life to the fullest extent.

v. Free yourself from regrets by accepting and dealing with past failure or adversity.

w. Do not hold a grudge or hate towards another.

x. Smile and laught at yourself

y. Live a healthy lifestyle where possible, if you intend being around for a while.

z. If you fail at a relationship…fail trying.

If the abovementioned is not your "cup of tea", I highly recommend that you involve your partner/spouse to chart down from a-z your own recipe for happiness.

CONCLUSION

"Finding Love"

"Finding Love"

Finding love is much easier than you think. In order to create money, you have got to have money. To create happiness, you have got to be happy…and so on.

In short, before you can search for or find love, you have to love the "Self". If you want intimate love, you have got to have some kind of idea of how you will deal with it once found. Many of us ask and sulk that we do not have this and do not have that…but once it is given, we either squander or waste it before the potential can be realized.

One sometimes only realises a good thing once it is gone. When encountering that potential person and learning of their past pain and torment, you think at the time…"how can anyone have given up such a wonderful person?"

When taking a closer look, we actually realize that one man's discarded penny is another's fortune. Look no further than the sidewalk. When I arrived here from South Africa, I noticed that people discard goods that are found in some of our stores back home where the average "Joe Soap" can shop.

Just realise the full potential in your partner or spouse before you decide to discard the relationship driven by menial differences that can be resolved. What would you do if met up with your ex and realized that what flourished in a new relationship was that same criteria you condemned the relationship? Would it be a bitter pill to swallow? Would you have regret? Or is it time you realise that different people bring out either good or bad in each other?

Accept this fact that we all have personal criteria and preferences that determine the partners we are with. If the differences extend beyond the probability rate or comparison, then be prepared for a short-lived relationship.

Finding true love can become an obsession that can cause much dissapointment and unhappiness for many. Nothing is going to fall in your lap if you do not work for it. Our reward comes from the fruit of our labour. What you put into a relationship, you will get out of and so it applies for all things we pursue in life.

If you are happy with yourself and feel you are a complete individual by knowing your goals, mistakes, shortcomings, and accepting them, you consistently re-invent yourself to become a better person. Then, you are well on your way to blend with and respect another individual with their unique traits that make them so special.

Let go of the notion to change or transform another to your liking or image and focus more on your ability to have tolerance for difference.

Through all this, know that nothing comes without faith-the ability to believe upon something not seen, yet hoped on.

SUMMARY

"If you have not Surrendered, you have not Loved."

"If you have not Surrendered, you have not Loved."

What is the message within this book regarding relationships?

The word "surrender" unfortunately indicates a sense of non-control that leaves us incapable to some extent. Surrender can be a great humanitarian endeavour. Look at warfare, a side normally surrendered due to the loss of life and assets. This surrender might not be a sign of weakness, but a sign of humanity to save lives and stop further suffering.

There is a difference between signing a peace treaty and surrendering. A peace treaty is a mutual agreement to uphold a peaceful resolution to prevent the outcome of loss. Surrender is the inevitable outcome of a situation in war. It is a forced resolution.

War is the trial and tribulation in a relationship. The outcome of such conditions can either lead to a defeat or victory, respectively, or to surrender by the fallen party. It is not what we surrender or give up for the sake of the relationship, but how we surrender to whom and if it is for the better or worse.

Our past hurt sometimes causes us to go into a relationship with certain conditions, and never in complete surrender in trust, truth, commitment, and love. We feel that if we give less of ourselves we will not loose as much. Although it is true to a large extent, realize that your partial input into the relationship will never give that sense of completeness to either be yourself or getting what you want. Once you determine that the partner you are with or aspire to be with has the same values, goals, and aspirations as you, there will be no need for surrender.

The surrender I am talking about in this book entails the ability to go into a relationship with a sense of freedom, with no conditions of extreme changes that force the relationship to be based on the constraints or limitations concerning trust, truth, respect, consideration, and love. If this feeling of sincere surrender is not mutual, by all means be cautious as to who you surrender to.

The persona of surrender does not entail the physical or intimate aspect of a relationship. That is a virtuous choice that solely relies upon one's personal and emotional ability to share all with another without concern.

Surrender also entails the full disclosure of one's past experiences that led up to the present. Understanding the good and bad in another can give you a clearer picture as to what you are getting yourself into. So, in short, surrender means full mutual disclosure of one's feelings and past experiences, leading to an open channel of commuication and set path to happiness and contentment.

If you are happy in your relationship, but seek motivation to overcome daily adversity and find strength through inspirational advice, read my next book on this subject.

I wish you well in whatever choice you make in your pursuit for Love, Commitment, Happiness, and Marriage. Just remember to stay true to yourself.

0-595-26888-9